COPYCAT
MARKETING
101

How To
Copycat
Your Way
To
Wealth

Burke Hedges

inti

Publishing

1

COPYCAT MARKETING 101
How to Copycat Your Way to Wealth

by Burke Hedges

Printed in the United States of America
First Edition, May 1997

ISBN 0-9632667-4-8

Published by INTI Publishing
Tampa, FL

Book cover designed by Cherry Design
Format and typography by Bayou Graphics

ALSO BY BURKE HEDGES

Who Stole the American Dream?

*You Can't Steal Second with Your
Foot on First!*

You, Inc.

*You, Inc. Audio Series
(6 audio cassettes and workbook)*

ACKNOWLEDGMENT

I'd like to thank the pioneers
of our industry
for blazing the trail
and mapping the path to success
for others to copycat.
Where would we be today
without your vision, courage,
and perseverance?

DEDICATION

*This book is dedicated to my parents
for providing a model of solid values and
hard work for me to copycat.*

CONTENTS

Introduction: *If You Don't Like Your Results,*
Change Your Approach! 1

Chapter 1: We Live in a World of
Copycats 9

Chapter 2: What Is "True" Wealth? 21

Chapter 3: Linear Growth:
Trading Time for Dollars 37

Chapter 4: Leveraged Growth:
Working Smarter, Not Harder 51

Chapter 5: Exponential Growth:
Formula for Building a Fortune 65

Chapter 6: Synergism: Marriages
Made in Heaven 77

Chapter 7: Network Marketing:
The Ultimate Copycat System! 89

Conclusion: *It's Your Turn!* 109

INTRODUCTION

If You Don't Like Your Results, Change Your Approach!

Introduction

If You Don't Like Your Results, Change Your Approach

There are two things needed these days: First, for rich people to find out how poor people live; and second, for poor people to find out how rich people work.

— John Foster

One of my favorite business stories is about a middle-aged manager struggling to pay his bills, so he decides to get some advice from a financial expert.

The manager makes an appointment to meet with a well-respected financial advisor whose office was located in a swanky building on Park Avenue.

The manager enters the expert's elegantly appointed reception room, but instead of a receptionist, the manager is greeted by two doors, one marked *"employed"* and the other *"self-employed."*

He enters the door marked "employed" and is greeted by two more doors, one marked *"makes less than $40,000"* and the other *"makes more than $40,000."*

He makes less than $40,000, so he enters that door, only to find himself face to face with two more doors. The door on the left is marked *"saves more than $2,000 a year,"* and the one on the right is marked *"saves less than $2,000 a year."*

The manager only has about a thousand dollars in his savings, so he enters the door on the right — only to find himself right back on Park Avenue!

THE SAME DOORS LEAD TO THE SAME RESULTS

It's painfully obvious that the manager in the story will never get out of his rut until he starts choosing to open different doors. The moral of the story is that most people are like the manager — they choose to enter the doors of life that lead them right back to where they started.

The only way for people to get different results is to choose to enter different doors, isn't that true? Like one of my mentors always used to say, *"If you continue to do what you've always done, you'll continue to get what you've always gotten."*

ARE YOU A 95%-ER? ... OR A 5%-ER?

Just like the manager in the story, most people are caught in a rut because they're trapped in an endless cycle of financial frustration.

Just like the manager in the story, 95% of the workers in most industrialized countries are employed ... they make less than $40,000 per year ... and they save about $2,000 per year.

At first glance, these figures look pretty impressive, especially to people who make less than $40,000. But the truth is, 95% of the people in this world aren't getting ahead — they're just getting by. Take a look at the financial condition of the "average" U.S. citizen at age 65:

100 TYPICAL AMERICANS AT AGE 65

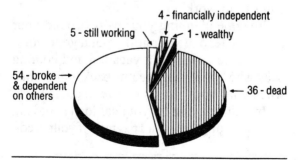

4 - financially independent
5 - still working
1 - wealthy
54 - broke & dependent on others
36 - dead

How about you? Are you opening financial doors that will lead to you becoming a 95%-er? Or are you opening the doors that will lead to financial independence, or even wealth, like the 5%-ers?

I've got to believe that most people want more for themselves ... more for their families ... than being dead, dead-broke, or still working to make ends meet by age 65. I've got to believe that if more people understood the full benefits of being a 5%-er, there would be a lot more people choosing to open different doors in their lives.

IMAGINE FOR A MOMENT ...

Imagine for a moment that time and money weren't an issue in your life.

Imagine being able to walk your kids to school every morning ... and never having to miss a school play or soccer game because you had to work.

Imagine planning your work around your golf ... instead of your golf around your work.

Imagine going on a vacation and coming back when you want to come back, rather than when your boss says you have to come back.

Imagine paying off your car loan ... paying off your mortgage ... and paying off your credit card bills at the end of every month.

Imagine that you are one of the 5%-ers, financially free to come and go as you please.

Finally, imagine that by investing one hour of your life reading this book, you will discover what you've always been searching for — the key to wealth creation!

The Purpose of This Book

Suppose you had the opportunity to become a 5%-er — would you take advantage of it?

I sincerely hope the answer to that question is "yes," because that's what this book is all about. In the coming pages you will learn that the secret to financial freedom is knowing which doors to open.

Copycat Marketing 101 will make you aware that most people are 95%-ers because they've been taught to copy people who are opening doors that lead to salary caps, dead-end jobs and financial dependence. *In short, most people are copycatting the wrong plan!*

In this book you will learn that the current system most people copycat is designed to create temporary income — not true wealth — because it's based on *linear growth* of trading time for dollars.

You will learn that the key to true wealth

creation is leverage, and you will learn about a dynamic form of leverage that wealthy people have been copying for centuries called *exponential growth*.

You will learn that the "secret" to wealth creation is available to virtually everybody, including people like you and me, because it's based on something that we already know how to do well — copycatting.

Best of all, you will learn how average people can break out of the time-for-money trap by copycatting a simple, duplicatable system of wealth creation that will open the door to financial freedom, once and for all!

CHAPTER 1

We Live in a World of Copycats

CHAPTER 1

We Live in a World of Copycats

Children have never been very good at listening to their elders. But they have never failed to imitate them.
— James Baldwin, author

One of the first books I remember reading as a kid was a joke book. I can still remember one of the corny jokes that used to crack up my friends and me: *It takes money to make money — you have to copy the design exactly.*

Hey, I told you it was a corny joke, didn't I? But the sentiment is dead serious.

Why haven't we found a way to copycat creating wealth?

Think about it — we copycat everything else in our lives, don't we? But the one thing we haven't learned to copycat is creating true wealth! Let's take a few moments to talk about the power of copycatting. And then we'll look at some of the reasons most people haven't found a way to copycat wealth creation.

ONE THING WE'RE ALL GOOD AT IS COPYCATTING

Each of us is blessed with certain talents and gifts that make us one-of-a-kind individuals. Some people are great dancers, while others can't tap their feet to the beat. Some of us have a talent for art, while others have trouble drawing a stick figure. Some of us are great athletes, while others can barely walk a straight line without stumbling.

But the one thing each and every one of us is good at — WITHOUT EXCEPTION — is copycatting.

Have you ever thought about how good we are at copycatting? When it comes to copycatting, we're all gifted. *We're copycat geniuses!* Copycatting is one trait we all excel at and that we all have in common, no matter where we live, no matter what our individual talents are. It makes no difference whether we are rich or poor ... black or white ... male or female ... the one thing we're all great at is copycatting.

So why haven't we found a way to copycat creating wealth?

COPYCATS FROM THE CRADLE TO THE GRAVE

Copycatting starts the day we are born. We copy the language we speak ... the food we eat ... the way we wear our hair ... the way we walk ... the way we dress.

When we enter school, we learn to read and write by copying letters in the alphabet. If you were born in a western culture, you copycatted the system of writing from the left side of the page to the right. If you were born in parts of Asia, you copycatted writing from the right to the left.

As we grew older, we learned to drive a car by copycatting, didn't we? The instructor showed us how to check the rearview mirror ... turn on the turn signal ... push slightly on the gas pedal ... drive the speed limit ... and come to a full stop at intersections. The better we were at copying our driving instructor, the easier it was to pass our driver's test.

WHEN IN ROME, DO AS THE ROMANS DO

We're so good at copycatting the people around us that we are often shocked by the customs and habits of people from different cultures. That's what the expression *"When in Rome, do what the Romans do"* is all about. It's a plain way of saying that we need to honor and respect different cultures, especially when we are visiting other countries.

But, that's a lot easier said than done. We get so comfortable with copycatting the customs around us that we're often amazed and amused when we hear what other cultures are copycatting. This short list of the favorite snacks of TV watchers around the world will show you just what I mean:

United States — popcorn

China — chicken feet

Japan — tea sandwiches

Mexico — ears of roasted corn

India — mutton sandwiches

Korea — sun-dried squid

Did you think to yourself, *"How could they eat THAT? Sun-dried squid? ... Chicken feet? ... You've got to be kidding!* But guess what you'd probably be snacking on while you watched TV if you grew up in Korea ... that's right, sun-dried squid.

COPYCATTING THE WAY WE WORK

Here's my point: There are countless differences between cultures, but the one thing every, single culture has in common is the way we go about learning the customs we practice — *we copycat!* We copycat so much that we take it for granted. Copycatting is so prevalent that it's second nature to us, like breathing air. So I ask you again, *Why haven't we found a way to copycat creating wealth?*

Make no mistake about it, copycatting is the most powerful learning tool known to humans! Copycatting impacts virtually every single phase of our lives, from our smallest habits to our biggest life-altering decisions.

For example, we spend a big part of our lives at work. Did you ever stop to consider how you learned to perform the tasks you perform at work? How did you learn to write a letter on the computer? How did you know what to wear to the office? And how did you teach others who were new on the job? By teaching them to copycat what you did, isn't that true? The psychologists call it "modeling and mirroring." I call it being a professional copycat!

No question, we copycat our way through life from the cradle to the grave because copycatting is easy to do ... we don't have to keep creating everything from scratch all the time ... it works ... and we're born geniuses at it! The expression *"Monkey see, monkey do"* could just as easily be *"People see, people do."*

That's why I say we live in a world of copycats. *If there's one thing every, single person in this world is good at — it's copycatting!*

A SHORT HISTORY LESSON ON COPYING JOBS

We even go so far as to copycat how we earn money. For thousands of years children of farmers copycatted their parents and became farmers ... children of shoemakers become shoemakers. That's why so many of our last names come from the trades, names like Farmer, Smith, Carpenter, Tailor, and so on.

With the advent of the Industrial Revolution, millions of children with last names like Farmer, Smith, Carpenter and Tailor broke away from the family trade and headed to the city to copycat a new concept of work — the job.

Copycatting the job worked pretty well for several generations, especially in America, the undisputed king of the Industrial Revolution. Because the first half of the 20th century was overshadowed by two world wars and the Great Depression, most people were overjoyed to copycat their family and friends and work a nine-to-five job. And as long as people's expectations didn't exceed their standard of living, people who copycatted the "gotta-get-a-job" mentality were content with what they had.

THINK BEFORE YOU COPYCAT

Like most everything in life, there's a flip side to copycatting. Just because we copycat something doesn't necessarily make it good ... or efficient ... or productive. Unfortunately, all too often copycatting is an excuse to get lazy in our thinking.

It reminds me of the story about the old shopkeeper on Main Street who placed a grand-father clock in the front window of his store. Over the years the shopkeeper noticed that a distinguished-looking man would walk by the store every day at noon ... pause in front of the grand-father clock ... pull out a pocket watch ... and carefully set the time.

One day the shopkeeper's curiosity got the best of him. When the gentleman paused in front of the grandfather clock, the shopkeeper ran out of the store and asked the man why he set his watch each and every day.

The man smiled and replied, *"I'm the fore-man at the town mill,"* he said. *"I blow the quitting whistle at 5:00 each day, and I want to be sure it goes off exactly on time."*

The old shopkeeper gave him a startled look — and then burst out laughing. The man stepped back and asked indignantly, *"What's so funny?"*

"I'm sorry," replied the shopkeeper. *"I didn't mean to be rude. But I just had to laugh. You see, all these years I've been setting my grand-father clock to your 5:00 whistle!"*

This story is a perfect illustration of the downside of copycatting. We copy others ... others copy us ... and all too often we *assume* that the people we are copying have the "right answer." I repeat, *we ASSUME we are copying the right people!*

That's exactly what happens when we take a job without really thinking about WHY we took the job. I think most people *assume* that jobs are the best way to create wealth, when in fact, jobs don't create *true wealth* — jobs create *temporary income.* And there's a big, BIG difference between the two.

LET'S RE-EXAMINE COPYCATTING THE JOB

Like I said earlier, copycatting is the most powerful learning tool known to humans. But every now and then we have to step back and *examine our assumptions* about what we are copying — and why — to make sure copycatting will, indeed, give us what we think it will give us.

Throughout this chapter I've repeatedly asked the question, *"Why haven't we found a way to copycat creating wealth?"* The answer is painfully obvious — most of us have been copycatting the job track instead of the wealth creation track.

Why? Because most people *assume* that a job is the only way to actualize their financial dreams. Perhaps they are unaware of alternatives to the job. Perhaps they don't believe there are other sources of wealth. Or perhaps they don't think they are capable of creating true wealth by working outside the job routine.

Whatever the reason, the result is the same. Most people become 95%-ers instead of 5%-ers because they are copycatting the job track and creating temporary income instead of true wealth.

What about you? What are you choosing to copycat? Are you choosing to be like 95% of the people who are copycatting the job track? ... Or are you choosing to be like the

5% who are copycatting the wealth creation track?

GET OFF YOUR ASSUMPTIONS!

As a wise person once observed, *"Your mind is like a parachute. It only works when it's open."* Today, more than ever before, it's imperative that we open our minds and become aware that jobs are a system for income creation, not wealth creation.

I believe that if people are serious about getting ahead in life — instead of just getting by — then they have to get off their assumptions and open their minds to alternative ways of creating wealth!

I believe that the 95%-ers — that is, people who continue to enter the door marked JOB — will continue to end up right back on the street where they started.

I believe, however, that if we are TRULY sincere about getting different results and becoming 5%-ers, we need to start entering doors that will open to wealth creation.

In the next chapter we'll talk more in depth about the difference between income creation and wealth creation — and we'll learn why true wealth is more attainable today than ever before in history!

CHAPTER 2

What Is "True" Wealth?

CHAPTER 2

What Is "True" Wealth?

If you have to tell people you're rich, you ain't.

— Joe E. Brown,
comedian

What does it mean to be wealthy — I mean, *truly* wealthy?

Certainly the word *wealth* means a lot of different things to a lot of different people. To me, wealth isn't just about being able to buy things, although that's a nice side benefit. To me, *true wealth* is synonymous with freedom.

Here's my personal definition of wealth — and I think it pretty much captures the biggest benefits of wealth:

> *Wealth is having enough money and enough time to do what you want, when you want.*

Do you think Bill Gates, who is worth billions,

keeps his job as CEO of Microsoft because he HAS to ... or because he WANTS to? I think it's safe to say that Bill Gates has enough money and enough time to do what he wants, when he wants, because Bill Gates has created *true* wealth, not just income. In a word, true wealth is freedom.

WEALTH MEANS FREEDOM TO CHOOSE

Chuck Feeney is in the same financial league as Bill Gates. As the founder of hundreds of duty-free shops in airports all over the world, Feeney is worth billions. Or I should say, he WAS worth billions. In 1984, Feeney donated 99.5% of his $3.5 billion fortune to a charitable foundation. Today he is donating his time and his money to worthy causes all over the world.

Both Bill Gates and Chuck Feeney understand that true wealth means having total freedom to choose how to spend your time ... and your money. Gates is choosing to spend his time creating more wealth, while Feeney is choosing to spend his time giving his fortune away. The common denominator that enables these two men to make two very different choices is *true* wealth.

SPEND YOUR TIME WISELY

Most people think true wealth is having lots

of money so you can buy material things. But the wisest people understand that true wealth isn't so much about *buying more things* as it is about *having more time to do what YOU want to do.*

Think about it. When you are old and gray, sitting on the front porch of a nursing home, contemplating how you lived your life, what are you most likely to regret — not buying a more expensive home? .... Or not spending more time with your kids when they were young?

What are you most likely to regret — not working around the clock for that promotion at the office? .... or not spending more time with your parents and your friends when they needed you?

Time is our most precious commodity — far more precious than gold — because once it's gone, you can never get it back! If you wreck your car, you can always buy another car. If you lose your job, you can always get another job. If you lose money in a bad investment, you can always make more money. But you can never, never get back the time you've lost or misspent, can you? Once it's gone, it's gone forever.

An ancient Chinese proverb says it best: *Better to throw all of your fortune down a deep*

well than to squander one moment of time.
That's why I say true wealth is having enough
money AND ENOUGH TIME to do what you
want, when you want. Without a doubt, the biggest benefit of true wealth is having the freedom to choose how you spend your time.

INCOME CREATION — THE TIME-FOR-MONEY TRAP

Have you ever known any hard-working
doctors or lawyers who make upwards of
$150,000 per year — *but they feel trapped?*
Are they creating true wealth? According to
my definition of wealth, the answer is *"no!"*

Here's why. Even though many highly paid
professionals have the *money* to buy and do what
they want, most *DO NOT have the time* because they HAVE TO keep working at their jobs,
day in and day out. In effect, they HAVE TO
work to create income so they can maintain their
lifestyles. People who are locked into their jobs
— no matter how much or how little they earn —
are victims of *income creation*, not *wealth creation*.

With *income creation*, you trade time for dollars, which means you don't earn the money until
you personally do the work. Whether it's a garbage collector earning the minimum wage of
$5.15 per hour ... or a heart surgeon earning
$5,000 per hour — income creation is still

trading a unit of time for a unit of dollars. With income creation, 10 hours of work equals 10 hours of pay.

Unfortunately, income creation is an endless treadmill. That's why I call income creation the time-for-money trap. Worst of all, when the treadmill stops, the income stops. Which means that workers who fall victim to illness ... or injury ... or long layoffs ... or burnout ... are income-less.

WHEN THE OUTGO EQUALS THE INCOME

Let's take a look at a typical "rich" professional — let's call him John Smith, M.D. — with an annual income of $150,000. Now, by almost everyone's standards, $150,000 a year is a lot of money. But when highly paid professionals become dependent on their incomes to support their lifestyles, they become unwitting victims of the time-for-money trap.

"TYPICAL" MONTHLY EXPENSES FOR A PROFESSIONAL EARNING $150,000 A YEAR		
Gross Income	$	150,000
33% tax bracket	$	50,000
Net Yearly Income	$	100,000
Monthly Income	**$**	**8,500**

(continued on next page)

Monthly Expenses

Loans for 2 luxury cars .... $	1,000
Mortgage on lakefront home .... $	2,000
Insurance: life, health, car .... $	500
2 kids in private school .... $	1,000
Dining out, entertainment; season tickets .... $	1,000
2 family vacations per year .... $	1,000
Clothing, jewelry, furniture .... $	500
Church, charity .... $	500
Country club dues .... $	500
Savings .... $	500
Total monthly "outgo" ....$	**8,500**
Monthly Income ....$	**8,500**
Money left over ....$	**—0—**

SLAVE TO TEMPORARY INCOME

As you can see, Dr. Smith lives a pretty nice lifestyle. We'd all love to have the money to join a swanky country club ... to take expensive ski vacations in Colorado or leisurely cruises in the Caribbean. Sure, Dr. Smith may have a lifestyle most of us only dream about, but he's paying a dear, dear price for that lifestyle because *he's mortgaged it with his freedom!*

You see, Dr. Smith has temporary income, but

he does NOT have the freedom to come and go as he pleases. He's chained to his job because he's become a slave to his lifestyle. Dr. Smith has to go to the office every day, whether he wants to or not. If Dr. Smith doesn't show up, he doesn't get paid. And if Dr. Smith doesn't get paid, neither does the mortgage ... or the car loans ... or the credit card bills ... or the tuition to private school. Is it any wonder that so many professionals fall victim to early heart attacks?

AN ACCIDENT WAITING TO HAPPEN

Where would the high-paid doctor be if he developed arthritis in his hands and could no longer create income because he had to stop working? More to the point, where would YOU be if you could no longer create income because you had to stop working? For most of us, that's the ultimate nightmare!

That's the problem with income creation — it's temporary. If you stop working, the income stops, too. And if you don't have any income stream other than your job, you're heading for disaster!

According to *Business Week* magazine, *"It takes the average worker half his lifetime to purchase a home, accumulate some savings and retirement benefits. It takes about six months of unemployment to lose it all."*

Scary, isn't it?

FREEDOM THROUGH RESIDUAL INCOME

Wouldn't it be great if you could enjoy all of the benefits of Dr. Smith's lifestyle without the liability of having to go into work if you don't want to? That would be the ultimate dream come true, wouldn't it?

Fortunately, there is another kind of income other than temporary income. It's called *residual income*, and unlike temporary income, residual income keeps earning money whether you show up to work or not! Residual income doesn't fall victim to the time-for-money trap because it is NOT dependent on trading time for dollars.

To see how residual income is created, let's look at another fictitious professional. We'll call him Joe Jones, CPA. Like, Dr. Smith, Mr. Jones has a thriving practice. But unlike Dr. Smith, Mr. Jones fully understood the power of residual income. For the last 40 years of his prosperous career, Mr. Jones saved 10% of his gross income and invested it wisely.

Now retired, today Mr. Jones has $1.5 million invested in mutual funds earning 10% per year, which gives him residual income equivalent to Dr. Smith's temporary income —

$150,000. Even though the incomes are the same, what each man has to do to earn it is very different, as the chart below indicates:

TEMPORARY INCOME	VS.	RESIDUAL INCOME
you trade time for dollars	↔	you leverage your time
money grows linearly	↔	money grows exponentially
income stops if you're disabled	↔	income continues indefinitely
you're not creating true wealth	↔	you're creating true wealth
time is not your own	↔	total time freedom
you're just getting by	↔	you're getting ahead
when work stops, income stops	↔	income keeps coming in

Now I ask you, which income would you prefer to receive — temporary income? ... or residual income? The answer is obvious.

CREATING TRUE WEALTH

Wealth creation — as opposed to income creation — isn't limited by the time-for-money trap because of a concept called leverage. The only way to create true wealth is to *leverage your time, money and efforts* so that 10 hours of work equals 100 hours of pay ... or even 1,000!

You see, the rich get richer because they take advantage of leverage by investing their money over time. As I pointed out in my second book, *You Can't Steal Second with Your Foot on First!*, the typical millionaire earned his fortune by saving 20% of his income and investing it wisely for years and years. That's the way the rich get rich and stay rich ... by putting their money to work for them by investing it over time.

That's the big difference between income creation and wealth creation. Income creation is temporary — you have to do the work or you don't get the income. Wealth creation is permanent — you escape the time-for-money trap by putting your money and your time to work for you.

LEVERAGING YOUR TIME

Now, I understand that very few people make enough — or are disciplined enough — to do what Mr. Jones, CPA, did and leverage his monthly savings into a million and a half dollars. Fortunately, leveraging your money is NOT the only tried-and-true way to create true wealth.

The other way to create true wealth is to leverage your time by investing it, instead of wasting it.

We've all used the expression, *Time is money*, haven't we? Well, due to the power of leverage, that axiom is truer today than ever before! It's obvious that we do NOT all have the same amount of money.

But it's equally obvious that we all DO have the same amount time. Now, I want you to understand that this book is NOT about investing your money to create wealth. It's about investing your time to create wealth because time equals money when you invest it properly!

It doesn't make any difference whether a person is a billionaire or a beggar, we all have access to the same amount of time: 24 hours in a day ... 168 hours in a week ... 672 hours in a month ... 8,064 hours in a year.

The key to wealth creation is NOT creating more time, which is impossible. The key is to take full advantage of the time we have, wouldn't you agree?

Fortunately for all of us, today there is a way to leverage some of our time (which we all have an equal amount of) to create true wealth, instead of leveraging our money (which most of us have very little of).

Fortunately, today there is a leveraged system where you can trade a little time for a lot of dollars ... instead of a linear system where you trade a lot of time for little dollars.

Fortunately, today there is a simple, duplicatable system for leveraging your time and efforts that virtually anyone can copycat.

ARE YOU COPYING THE WRONG SYSTEM?

Let's face it, most of us weren't born with the last name of DuPont or Rockefeller. We aren't born geniuses, like Bill Gates and Chuck Feeney. And we don't have the talent of Michael Jordan or Tom Cruise.

All too often we assume that wealth creation comes from winning the lottery of life — it's only meant for super-talented people ... or super-blessed people ... but it's certainly not meant for average people, like you and me.

THAT'S NONSENSE!

We must not buy in to that line of limited thinking. That's garbage thinking, and we need to throw that kind of negative thinking out with the trash, starting right now!

The truth is that most people *assume* they can't create wealth *when, in fact, they can!* The real reason most people don't create true wealth is because they've never been made aware of a wealth-creating system they can copy. In other words, most of us have bought into copycatting the wrong plan. Because we aren't aware of a wealth-building model to copy, we copy what everyone else we know is doing — we take a job! We do what most people do ... and as a result, we get what most people get!

NOT KNOCKING JOBS

Please understand that I am NOT knocking jobs. I'm knocking the RESULTS we get from working at a job. If jobs created true wealth, I'd be the first person to tell you to follow the job track. But they don't — that's just the cold, hard reality of it all!

COPYCAT EXPONENTIAL GROWTH, NOT LINEAR GROWTH

Truth is, you will never create true wealth as long as you are copycatting the income creation system because it's based on *linear growth* as opposed to wealth creation, which is based on *leveraged growth*.

In the next chapter we will take a closer look at the limitations of linear growth, and we'll discuss why we need to start copycatting leveraged systems if we are sincere about becoming totally free by creating true wealth.

CHAPTER 3

Linear Growth:
Trading Time for Dollars

CHAPTER 3

Linear Growth: Trading Time for Dollars

Work all day,
Live on hay.
When you die,
Pie in the sky.

— Joe Hill,
1920s union organizer

I used to tell people in my seminars that most workers are on the 40/40/40 plan — they work 40 hours a week ... for 40 years ... and then when they retire, they get a retirement dinner and a $40 watch!

But like a lot of things in our fast-changing world, the 40/40/40 plan is outdated. Today most of us are on the 50/50/50/50 plan. Nowadays we work *50 hours a week ... 50 weeks a year ... for 50 years ... and then retire on 50%*

of what we can't live on today!

TIME-FOR-MONEY TREADMILL

The 50/50/50/50 plan is the classic example of *income creation* because it's based on *linear growth*. The math to calculate linear growth income is very simple:

H *(hourly wage)* **x N** *(number hours worked)* **= I** *(income)*

The definition of *linear* is "the outcome is proportional to the input." In layman's terms, that means you get out what you put in — nothing more, nothing less. In linear income growth, one unit of time equals one unit of money. As a result, the only way to increase income based on linear growth is to work more hours or get a raise.

Now, at first glance, linear growth seems pretty fair. It rewards people who are paid a good hourly salary and are willing to put in the hours. But the problem with workers earning income based on linear growth is that they'll always have a cap on their income, no matter how much they earn per hour.

THE PAINTER AND THE PROFESSIONAL

To best illustrate the limitations of linear growth, let's look at two acquaintances of

mine with two very different occupations —
a house painter and a doctor.

The painter's name is Gary, and he owns a
small painting and wallpapering business near
my home in Clearwater, Florida. Gary works
hard. He's on the job early and he works until dark. He works weekends when he can.

When Gary bids out a job, he figures his
rate at $12 per hour. But after factoring in
travel time, trips to the hardware store and so
on, it's probably closer to $10 an hour. If Gary
is lucky enough to work 10 hours a day, six
days a week, here's what he will earn in a year:

  1 x $10 = *$10 per hour*
  60 hours per week = *$600 per week*
  50 weeks per year = *$30,000 per year*

Now, $30,000 per year is nothing to sneeze
at. A lot of people would love to make
$30,000 a year. But that's the most Gary will
gross in a great year, when one good job fol-
lows another. But look at the price Gary has
to pay for a great year:

✓ He only gets to spend one day a week with
  his wife and kids.

✓ He'll never make more than $30,000 a
  year, no matter how hard he works.

✓ He seldom gets time off, and when he does, he's too tired (or too broke) to enjoy it!

✓ Here's the worst part of working for income based on linear growth: *Gary only gets paid <u>once</u> for the work he's done.* Which means once he gets his last paycheck, he's back on the time-for-money treadmill.

PROFESSIONALS: NOTHING MORE THAN HIGH-PRICED HOUSE PAINTERS

Now let's go back and revisit John Smith, M.D., who earns $150,000 a year in his medical practice. Dr. Smith is a general practitioner with his own private practice. Although two of his four full-time employees are registered nurses, Dr. Smith must see his patients in person. So he works eight hours a day, six days a week attending to patients ... then spends two additional hours a day filling out paperwork ... and spends two Sundays of each month on business matters.

The only way Dr. Smith can increase his income is by increasing his hours. But because he's already working 10-hour days, by the time he gets home he's too exhausted to help the kids with homework or attend his son's soccer games — much less add more time to his work day.

A SLAVE TO HIS JOB

True, Dr. Smith makes a lot of money. But the trade-off is he's a P.O.W. — a Prisoner Of Work! He feels trapped! He's frustrated ... angry ... and unhappy ... but he doesn't know what to do about it. So he just keeps going back into the salt mines, trading time for dollars, hoping that things will get better — but knowing in his heart they won't!

That's the problem with income based on linear growth — if you're not personally doing the work, the work doesn't get done. If the work doesn't get done, you don't get paid. And the only way to get paid is to keep doing the work over and over again. Heaven forbid the painter or the doctor ever gets sick or injured and can't go to work!

WHAT DOES YOUR TREADMILL PAY?

What about you — are you on the time-for-money treadmill? If so, how much does your treadmill pay? Below is a list of occupations and their average yearly salary, as reported by *Parade Magazine* in its annual report, *"What People Earn."* Take a look at how your yearly compensation compares to other occupations:

1996 AVERAGE SALARIES FOR JOBS IN USA*

Occupation	*Annual Salary*
Hospital Janitor	$ 17,000
High School Teacher	$ 33,500
Corporate Attorney	$ 85,500
Secretary	$ 16,000
Sales Clerk	$ 10,000
President of United States	$ 200,000
Newspaper Reporter	$ 32,000
Travel Agent	$ 28,000
Physician	$ 141,000
Minister	$ 23,500
Accountant	$ 39,000

*Average household income for family in U.S. — $38,962

Were you surprised at how your income compares to the incomes of other jobs around the country? Well, you're in for an even bigger surprise when you compare your yearly salary to the compensation for a CEO of a large company.

Just take a look at how CEO pay compares to the pay of an average worker in 1996:

WAGE GAP BETWEEN CEO AND WORKERS

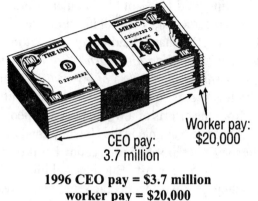

Worker pay:
$20,000

CEO pay:
3.7 million

**1996 CEO pay = $3.7 million
worker pay = $20,000
ratio = 187 to 1**

Isn't it amazing how one person at a company can be worth $3.7 million, while the rank-and-file worker at the same company is worth only $20,000? *How can that be?* you may ask yourself.

BREAKING THE TIME-FOR-MONEY TRAP WITH LEVERAGE

I can answer your question in one word — LEVERAGE. You see, when a typical worker trades his time for dollars, his income is growing in a linear fashion. One unit of time equals one unit of money. The worker is earning 100% of his own, singular efforts.

The CEO, on the other hand, leverages his

time and talents through his employees. Instead of getting paid 100% of his singular efforts, he makes a percentage of all of his employees' efforts. That's what J. Paul Getty was getting at when he said, *"I'd rather earn 1% of 100 men's efforts rather than 100% of my own."* That's why leverage is so powerful — you earn a little bit from the efforts of a whole bunch of people.

A classic example is the Hershey candy bar. Hershey's net profit on each candy bar is only a penny or two, at most. But they sell billions of Hershey bars worldwide each and every year. That's why the makers of Hershey candy bars, Mars, Inc., is able to post profits of a billion plus dollars a year, year in and year out. And that's why the CEO of Hershey makes big, BIG bucks!

THE HERMIT AND THE CHAIN SAW

The concept of leverage is like the story of the hermit and the chain saw. One day an old hermit came down from his cave in the mountain to buy a saw at the local hardware store.

"I'm movin' out of my cave and building myself a new log home," the hermit proudly announced to the young sales clerk. *"I need the best saw you got — and price is not an object."*

The young sales clerk disappeared into the warehouse for a moment before returning with a gleaming new chain saw. *"This is the best saw on the market,"* the sales clerk said confidently. *"It will cut through trees like a knife through butter. I guarantee it will cut a month's worth of lumber in a day — or I'll personally refund your money from my paycheck!"*

The excited hermit paid the clerk, grabbed his gleaming new chain saw by the handle and headed back up the mountain.

Exactly one month later the young clerk was busy stocking shelves when he heard the hermit's voice crack through the air like a whip. *"Hey, Sonny, I've come to return this saw and get my money back, like you promised."*

The clerk looked up to see the old hermit — but was shocked at what he saw! The hermit looked like he hadn't slept in weeks. His clothes were shreaded and stained with blood and sweat. He looked like he'd been worked half to death.

"Wh-Wh-what happened to you?" the clerk stammered. *"You look terrible!"*

The old hermit summoned all his strength and lifted his chain saw onto the counter, grumbling, *"It's this dadburn saw you sold me. You said it'd cut a month's worth of lumber in a day. Well, I've been using this contraption for 30 days now, and I ain't even been able to cut a day's worth of lumber in a month. I want my money back!"*

The startled clerk apologized and said, *"Sure, a deal's a deal. Just let me have a look at this saw for you. Maybe I can figure out what's wrong."*

The clerk gave the pull rope a quick yank ... and the chainsaw exploded into a roar — **"B-R-R-R-R-R-R-R-R!!"**

The hermit jumped back from the counter like he'd been shot, shouting over the roaring saw, **"WHAT'S THAT SOUND?"**

A LESSON ABOUT LEVERAGE

Can you imagine trying to cut down a tree with a chain saw that wasn't even turned on? No wonder the hermit looked beat up and worn out. The story brings home the point that leverage is an awesome tool, but only if we put it to use.

The chain saw is obviously a great tool for leveraging time and effort. If you've ever tried to cut up a big tree limb using a hand saw, you know exactly what I mean. The irony of the story is the hermit had in his hands a powerful tool for leverage. He just didn't know how to use it! In other words, his failure didn't result from a lack of talent or effort. *His failure resulted from a lack of knowledge!*

The same can be said for the average person. Through the power of leverage, we can accomplish our goals in a fraction of the time with a fraction of the effort. We can, in effect, "cut a month's worth of lumber in a day." But in order to take full advantage of leverage, we have to have the knowledge that it exits. Otherwise, we'll end up like the hermit — we'll still try to get ahead *working harder* trading time for dollars, instead of *working smarter* by leveraging our time and efforts.

Isn't this why by age 65, the average person will be dead ... dead broke ... or dependent on the state, family or church — too many people are copycatting a linear plan instead of a leveraged plan?

Knowledge Is the First Step

By copying the right kind of leverage in the right situation, we can move mountains ... and we can make millions.

The question is, *"What system of wealth creation do you want to copycat?"*

Do you want to continue to copycat the linear system of wealth creation and end up like the old hermit, trading lots of effort for very little return?

Or would you like to be like the young clerk and learn how to turn on the chain saw of leverage?

That's what you will learn in the next chapter — proven ways we can leverage our time and efforts so that we break out of the time-for-money trap — FOREVER — and claim the financial independence that we deserve.

CHAPTER 4

Leveraged Growth:
Working Smarter, Not Harder

CHAPTER 4

Leveraged Growth:
Working Smarter, Not Harder

*It is not enough to be busy; so
are the ants. The question is:
What are we busy about?*
— Henry David Thoreau

I n August of 1888, an Atlanta druggist by
the name of Asa Candler paid $2,300 in cash
for the exclusive rights to a carbonated fountain
drink called Coca-Cola.

Coca-Cola was an immediate success in the
Atlanta area, and by the turn of the century virtually every drug store in the South featured a
soda fountain where a customer could sit down
and sip a cold Coke for 5 cents.

Then Candler made a monumental decision
that would transform Coca-Cola from a small

regional company into an international house-hold name. Candler decided his company could make more money with less time and effort by introducing a unique form of leverage — *bottling*!

THE SECRET TO COKE'S INTERNATIONAL SUCCESS

There's a fascinating story behind Candler's decision to bottle coke. Legend has it that a good friend burst into Candler's office one day and proclaimed that, for a hefty fee, he would let Candler in on the secret for vastly expanding Coca-Cola's profits.

The two men bickered back and forth for a good part of the day until Candler's curiosity eventually got the best of him, and he wrote his friend a check. The friend graciously accepted the check and then leaned forward and whispered in Candler's ear two simple words that launched a global dynasty: *Bottle it!* Fortunately, Candler had the vision to take his friend's advice. And the rest, as they say, is history.

LEVERAGING TIME AND LOCATION

Bottle it!

Just think for a moment about the power of these words. Before Coke came in bottles, you had to go to the local soda fountain to order a

Coke — or you had to go without. Before bottling, Coke sales could only grow as the number of soda fountains grew.

Bottling changed all that. The consumer didn't have to go to the soda fountain to enjoy a Coke because, in effect, when a consumer bought a six-pack of coke, the consumer brought the soda fountain home with him!

As a result, today virtually anyone in the world can enjoy a refreshing drink of Coca-Cola in the convenience of their home, anytime of the day or night. All because the Coca-Cola Company had the wisdom to *leverage* time, effort and location by bottling their product.

WHAT IS LEVERAGE?

The root word of leverage — *lever* — comes from an old French word meaning "to make lighter," which is an apt description of the power of leverage. By wisely using certain levers or tools, difficult tasks can be performed in a lot less time with a lot less effort, thus making them "lighter."

Consider the effort it would take to replace an engine in a car without taking advantage of leverage. How many strong men do you think it would take to lift an engine out of your car — 5? 10? More?

Now think about how your local car mechanic

could perform the same task in a fraction of the time with a fraction of the effort. First he'd position a well-oiled hoist on a sturdy beam above the engine. Next he'd secure the engine with ropes and chains attached to the hoist. Then he'd attach the pull rope to an electric-powered fly wheel. With a flick of a switch, the engine could be lifted out of the car in a matter of seconds.

That's the power of leverage — it increases productivity by maximizing time, effort and money.

HOW CORPORATIONS USE LEVERAGE

For centuries enterprising people have been making their jobs "lighter" — that is, more productive and more profitable — through the concept of leverage. That's really what increased productivity is all about — working smarter instead of harder by finding a way to make a lot more money in a lot less time.

Hiring employees is the most obvious way business owners leverage their time. Virtually every major company in the world — from Ford Motor Company to Sony — started off with a sole proprietor who leveraged his time and talents through employees.

If Henry Ford, for example, had built the Model T by himself, he could have pocketed

100% of the profits. But he knew he'd only be able to build a car or two each year working solo. Ford was smart enough to leverage his time and talents by teaching his employees to copycat his system. By taking advantage of the power of leverage, Ford built thousands of cars each year — and became one of the richest men in history!

GETTING REAL SMART SELLING REAL ESTATE

Real estate companies have been taking advantage of the leverage concept for years, but instead of leveraging employees, a realtor leverages a team of independent contractors (better known as real estate agents).

Let's look at how a hypothetical real estate professional named Ted uses leverage to make more money in less time. Ted has been selling real estate for 20 years or so. When he first started out, he was lucky to sell one house a month. But over the years Ted got better at his job. After five years in the business, he would sell 50 houses a year on average.

But no matter how hard Ted worked, it was impossible for him to sell more than one house a week by himself. After all, he could only show so many houses in a day. He could only go to so many closings in a week. So he decided to open an office.

Ted recruited some of his realtor friends to work out of his office. Over the years he assembled 20 top-notch real estate agents. Each one of those agents sold 50 houses a year, which meant his office was selling more than 1,000 houses a year!

Now, just look at what leverage has done for Ted. On his own, Ted could sell 50 houses. By leveraging the time and talents of other agents, Ted could sell 1,000 houses — which would be impossible if he were still working alone. By using leverage, he is 20 times more productive while working fewer hours. That's what the expression *"working smarter, not harder"* is all about!

LEVERAGING THROUGH FRANCHISING

Franchising took the concept of leverage to an even higher level than a real estate office. Although franchising has been around for years, it wasn't recognized as a "legitimate" business concept until the early 1950s, when a milk shake appliance salesman named Ray Kroc bought the rights to franchise a fast-food restaurant called McDonald's.

Ray Kroc didn't invent franchising. But he sure perfected it. Kroc understood that the key to a successful franchise was duplication. So he went about setting up a fool-proof system that spelled out every detail of a successful franchise. He even went so far as to spend $3 million to research the secret of consistently perfect french fries. When someone bought a McDonald's franchise, all they had to do was connect the dots. It was a copycatter's dream come true!

Think about this — when you enter a McDonald's, where is the french fry machine? On the left, isn't it? It doesn't make any difference whether the franchise is in Moscow, Idaho, or Moscow, Russia, the french fry machine is on the left. And you better believe every other detail of the operation is spelled out and in the right place, too.

Duplication: The Key to Successful Franchising

The concept of franchising works so well because it is so simple — brilliantly simple. It's a classic win/win situation where both the franchisor and the franchisee come out way ahead.

Through trial and error, the *franchisor* develops a duplicatable business model built around a proven product (like Domino's pizza) or a needed service (like Kinko's copier service).

The key to becoming a successful franchisor is to develop a successful system and then record what needs to be done in detail so that the model can be taught to somebody else.

If a model is proven and can be copycatted by the average person, then it can be success-fully franchised. If, however, the success of the model depends on the talent of a one-in-a-million "star," then it can't be successfully franchised because the star can't be duplicated.

"STARS" ARE NOT DUPLICATABLE

The reason the actor Tom Cruise can com-mand $20 million a picture is because he's the essence of a star. In Hollywood terms, he's "bankable." When Tom Cruise stars in a movie, it's almost guaranteed the movie will make money — BIG money!

You can't, however, franchise the product "Tom Cruise," because he's not duplicatable. The average person can't copy what Tom Cruise does and expect the same results. That's why you can't franchise creative endeavors, like writ-ing a best-selling book or singing a hit song. Because they depend on the star factor, they are unique and can't be copycatted.

Some products and businesses, however, are easily duplicatable. Pizza is the perfect example.

The ingredients are plentiful and inexpensive. It only takes a few minutes to turn out a perfect product. And virtually anyone with a high school education (or less) and a desire to get ahead can learn to copycat the franchise model for Pizza Hut or Domino's. Let's face it, a franchisee doesn't have to be a rocket scientist. But he does have to be a great copycatter of a proven system.

FROM ZERO TO HERO

Does the concept of leveraging time and money through duplication work? To answer that question, all you have to do is look at what has happened to franchising over the last 50 years. When Ray Kroc started duplicating his operation, most people considered franchising a "scam." The United States Congress even tried to outlaw it.

Ironically, the perception of franchising has taken a 180-degree turn since the early days. Experts estimate that today anywhere from 34% to 60% of the goods and services in America are distributed through franchising, and savvy investors all over the world are paying millions of dollars for the right to copycat a proven franchise.

The brilliance behind franchising's phenomenal success is the concept of duplication through copycatting. The downside to franchising, however, is the start-up cost. Let's face it, very few people have a million dollars to plunk down for a McDonald's franchise. To complicate matters, you must own and operate multiple franchises to become truly wealthy in a franchise system.

THE ALTERNATIVE FRANCHISE: ™ THE ULTIMATE COPYCAT SYSTEM

Suppose there were a franchise-type concept with a very affordable start-up cost of $500 or less. And suppose this "alternative franchise"™ took advantage of the most powerful form of leveraged growth known to humans — *exponential growth* through compounding. What you would have is the ultimate copycat system to create wealth, wouldn't you?

Today there is a way for the average person to copycat the wealth-building system of history's richest people.

Today there is a way to get paid 1,000 times for the work you do once, instead of getting paid once for the work you do 1,000 times.

In the coming pages you're going to learn more about exponential growth, a proven system for wealth creation that average people like you and I can copycat. And you'll learn how the combination of exponential growth and the franchise concept can empower you to create more personal wealth in less time than any other income system available today!

CHAPTER 5

Exponential Growth:
Formula for Building a Fortune

CHAPTER 5

Exponential Growth: Formula for Building a Fortune

If you want to get rich, just find someone making lots of money and do what he's doing.

— J. Paul Getty

I'd like to open this chapter by telling you a story about an 88-year-old washerwoman named Oseola McCarty. This story will open your eyes to the most powerful, most democratic form of wealth-building leverage in the world. It's called *compounding*, and it has the power to transform paupers into princes.

TOUGH LIFE

Oseola McCarty has lived a tough life, that's for sure. At age eight she was forced to drop out of second grade to help her mother wash and iron the neighbors' clothes. Seventy years later, Oseola was still working as a washer-woman.

She charged $1.50 to $2 a bundle — that's a week's worth of laundry for a family of four — until the end of WWII. After the war she increased her price to $10 per bundle. Even in her best year, working 10 hours a day, six days a week, Oseola never earned more than $9,000.

SMALL SAVINGS MAKE A BIG DIFFERENCE

Oseola was 40 years old when she was finally able to start saving money. She squirreled away pennies and nickles at first ... then quarters ... and eventually dollar bills. She put her savings in a local bank and never touched it. Over time, her savings added up, and the principle and interest on those savings kept building and building.

In the summer of 1995, Oseola McCarty — the elementary school drop-out who never earned more than $9,000 a year — *donated $150,000 to the University of Southern Mississippi!*

COMPOUNDING: 8TH WONDER OF THE WORLD

How is it that an average woman with below-average education and income can accumulate a small fortune? In Oseola's own words, *"The secret to building a fortune is compounding interest."*

Webster's defines compound interest as "the interest paid on both the principle and the accumulated unpaid interest." The key word in this definition is "accumulated." If the principle or interest is spent instead of reinvested, the power of compounding is diminished.

Also known as the "doubling concept," compounding has created more fortunes than any other single investment vehicle in history. With compounding, your money is working for you, even when you're not working. Albert Einstein, a man who knew a thing or two about mathematics, went so far as to call compounding "the 8th wonder of the world." Indeed, compounding is the wealth creation principle that drives Wall Street and the banking industry.

EXPONENTIAL GROWTH = EXPLOSIVE GROWTH

What is it about compounding that makes it the "8th wonder of the world?" What property of compounding enables it to turn meager savings into small fortunes? The answer is *exponential growth*, the ultimate tool for leveraging time and money!

In Chapter 3, you'll remember, we talked about the limitations of linear growth. To best understand the dramatic difference between exponential growth and linear growth, let's take a moment to review some basic principles of arithmetic that we first learned about in middle school.

Linear refers to certain functions of basic math, like simple addition. A typical *linear equation* would look like this:

$$5 + 5 = 10$$

Linear gets its name because the growth occurs in a straight line, step by step. That's why we refer to linear equations as calculations in "the first power only."

Exponential, on the other hand, refers to a more sophisticated form of multiplication known as "squaring." A typical *exponential equation* might look like this:

$$5^2 = 25$$
(vs. the linear equation $5 + 5 = 10$)

Exponential gets its name from the small number placed above and to the right of another number to indicate how many times the root number should be multiplied by itself. That's why we refer to exponential equations as calculations in "the second power" or "third power," and so on.

The bottom line is this. Linear growth is incremental and gradual. Exponential growth is drastic and dramatic. Here's a simple equation to always keep in mind when you are investing your money ... or your time:

"Linear Equals Limited.
Exponential Equals Explosive."

THE RULE OF 72

To better understand the awesome power of exponential growth, let's look at a doubling concept called the *Rule of 72*. The Rule of 72 is a simple formula for figuring out how long it will take for an investment to double.

Here's how it works: To calculate how many years it will take for your investment money to double, first you determine the annual interest rate. Then divide that interest rate into 72. The number you end up with is the number of years it will take for your investment to double.

For example, let's say you invest $10,000 in a stock that pays you an annual return of 10% (the average annual return in the stock market for the last 50 years).

RULE OF 72 IN ACTION

$10,000 original investment
10% return on investment
$72 \div 10 = 7.2$ years

Therefore, it will take 7.2 years for your investment of $10,000 to double into $20,000.

The Rule of 72 is certainly simple to calculate, but the results of the formula are nothing short of miraculous. The chart below compares a $10,000 investment growing linearly vs. exponentially at 10% per year (remember, at 10%, $10,000 will double every 7.2 years).

	Linear Growth (simple addition concept)	Exponential Growth (doubling concept)
investment:	$10,000	$ 10,000
after 7 yrs:	$10K + $10K = $20,000	$ 20,000
after 14 yrs:	$20K + $10K = $30,000	$ 40,000
after 22 yrs:	$30K + $10K = $40,000	$ 80,000
after 29 yrs:	$40K + $10K = $50,000	$ 160,000
after 36 yrs:	$50K + $10K = $60,000	$ 320,000
after 43 yrs:	$60K + $10K = $70,000	$ 640,000
after 50 yrs:	$70K + $10K = $80,000	$ 1,300,000

This chart is a vivid illustration of the power of exponential growth — and it points out the serious limitations of linear growth. The first few years the growth is about the same. But because exponential growth occurs geometrically, the growth of the investment becomes more and more explosive over time. The final total tells the tale — *$80,000 generated by lin-*

*ear growth, as opposed to $1.3 million gener-
ated by exponential growth!*

That's why I call exponential growth "the
formula for building a fortune." Exponential
growth enables your money to grow in mul-
tiples, instead of growing in a measured, step-
by-step pace.

COMPOUNDING YOUR WAY TO WEALTH

A perfect example of the power of exponential growth through compounding is the investment fund founded by one of the world's richest men, Warren Buffett. If you had invested
$10,000 with Buffett's Berkshire Hathaway
Fund in 1956 and reinvested the interest and
dividends year after year, today your investment
would be worth $80 million!

Sounds impossible, doesn't it? ... An $80 mil-
lion return on an investment of only $10,000!
But that's the power of taking advantage of compounding by letting your investment grow year
after year. Just look at a few of the companies
that have grown 100-fold over the years: Xerox
... Kodak ... IBM ... Wal-Mart ... Microsoft ...
just to name a few. If you had the foresight ...
the patience ... and the money to invest with any
one of these companies 25 years ago, you'd be
a millionaire many times over today.

LEVERAGE FOR THE LITTLE GUY

Oseola McCarty is a classic example of why I call compounding *"leverage for the little guy."* The two other kinds of leverage I talked about in the last chapter — employees and franchising — are certainly powerful tools for leveraging. But you need either lots of money or lots of talent to put them to use.

On the other hand, virtually anyone can take advantage of the awesome power of compounding. Compounding is the backbone of the exponential system of wealth creation, a dynamic way for you to leverage your time, talents, efforts and money.

The copycat system you're going to learn in the coming pages eliminates the two biggest drawbacks to compounding — time and money. Let me explain. Most people today don't have $100,000 ... or $50,000 ... or even $10,000 lying around to invest. And even if they did, they aren't willing to wait 40 to 50 years for it to grow exponentially. With the cost of living going through the roof, two-income families can barely make ends meet, much less invest their hard-earned money in the hopes of living long enough to enjoy a cushy retirement.

TIME IS MONEY

So the question becomes "How can you create wealth through exponential growth without having to invest thousands of dollars ... or without having to wait a lifetime while your small nest egg doubles itself into a small fortune?" The answer to that question can be found in an affordable, duplicatable concept that combines franchising with exponential growth. It's called Network Marketing.

It's true that most people in this world don't have much money. But one thing we all have is time. Let's face it, all of us can reorganize our day to squeeze out a few more hours if we're serious about using that time to start creating true wealth.

Here's a simple formula for success in the coming decades:

T = time invested in duplicating
　　　a copycat model (franchise concept)
E^2 = exponential growth
$\$$ = financial freedom

$$T \times E^2 = \$$$

In the pages that follow, you are going to learn how Network Marketing will enable you to copycat your way to wealth by investing your time ... instead of your money.

The question isn't whether or not this simple, duplicatable system for creating true wealth works. It works, all right, as evidenced by thousands upon thousands of financially free men and women working in a $100 billion worldwide industry growing at a rate of 10% a year.

The question, my friend, isn't whether or not this proven system works. The question is this: *"Do you have the vision to see it ... the wisdom to understand it ... and the courage to take advantage of it so that you, too, can copycat your way to wealth?"*

CHAPTER 6

**Synergism: Marriages
Made in Heaven**

CHAPTER 6

Synergism:
Marriages Made in Heaven

*If you have built castles in the air,
your work need not be lost. That is
where they should be. Now put the
foundations under them.*

— Henry David Thoreau

A determined immigrant named Ernest Hamwi was trying his best to sell paper-thin Persian waffles at the 1905 World's Fair. He worked from sun up to sun down ... he gave away free samples to everyone who walked past his waffle stand ... but nothing seemed to work. No one wanted to buy his waffles.

To make matters worse, day after day thousands of hot, hungry fair-goers would rush past Ernest's lonely waffle booth on their way to stand in line at the ice cream booth two doors down. Ernest would spend his long days watching the ice cream vendor rake in money hand over fist. Talk about adding insult to injury!

On one especially hot, crowded afternoon, Ernest's fortune took a sudden turn for the better. The ice cream was selling so fast that the vendor ran out of dishes. In desperation, he ran down to Ernest's waffle stand, begging for extra plates.

A MARRIAGE MADE IN HEAVEN

Ernest didn't have any plates. All he had were stacks and stacks of soft, sweet Persian waffles that he couldn't even give away. Suddenly, Ernest had an idea. Maybe he could roll one of his waffles up into a cone that would hold a scoop of ice cream. Sure enough, the cone worked like a charm — and that was the beginning of the world's love affair with the ice cream cone.

Ice cream and Ernest's waffle cone went together like a horse and carriage. It was a marriage made in heaven. The ice cream cone became an overnight sensation and the hit of the 1905 World's Fair. Nearly a century later, ice cream cones are still the world's favorite dessert.

The ice cream story is a great example of the concept of *synergism*. That is, the combination of two different products or concepts is often greater than the sum of its parts. The ice cream cone is creative synergism in action:

Ice cream tastes good.

Waffles taste good.

Put them together — THEY TASTE GREAT!

THE AWESOME POWER OF CREATIVE SYNERGISM

History is filled with incidents where the synergism of two distinctly different concepts created breakthrough products ... incredibly profitable enterprises ... and huge opportunities!

One of my favorite synergism stories led to the best-selling product in the history of a major Fortune 500 company, the 3M Corporation. A 3M employee was looking for a way to keep his bookmark from falling out of his hymn book during church choir practice.

He explained his problem during a brainstorming meeting at the office. A chemical engineer remembered a failed experiment with a new adhesive, and suggested applying it to the back of a notepad. That unlikely marriage between a notepad and a failed adhesive ended up becoming the Post-It Note®, a product that produces billions of dollars in revenues for 3M each and every year!

THE SECRET TO SUCCESSFUL SYNERGISM

The key to a successful synergism is to create an entirely new product or service by combining two seemingly unrelated concepts. Many times synergisms are a matter of luck, as was the case with the invention of the ice cream cone. Other times synergisms are the result of some very creative people thinking "out of the box." Whatever the cause, the effect of a successful synergism is powerful ... unexpected ... explosive ... and life-altering.

Let's take a brief look at four modern-day synergisms that have dramatically impacted the lives of people all over the world:

The Automobile — If a worldwide survey asked people to name the invention that most symbolized the 20th century, most people would likely say the automobile. By *synergistically combining the horse-drawn carriage with the internal combustion engine*, Karl Benz in Germany and Henry Ford in America chauffeured in the modern age.

The Fax Machine — Can you imagine doing

business without a fax machine? With the exception of the telephone, the fax may be the single most affordable and efficient business tool available today. The fax is the perfect example of creative synergism, *a combination of the telephone and the copier.* What a great concept ... and what a marvelous convenience.

The Personal Computer — The PC is the ultimate synergistic product, a *brilliant combination of the calculator and the typewriter.* In the early 1960s, Steven Jobs, co-founder of Apple Computer, had a vision. He saw a day in the not-too-distant future when there would be a small, inexpensive, incredibly powerful computer sitting atop every desk in every home, office, and school in the world. The PC is synergism at its best!

Franchising — It could be argued that franchising is the most successful business model of the 20th century. Franchising is the synergistic *combination of the successful chain store, like Sears, and the small business owner.* The concept has been so successful over the last 50 years that today some experts estimate more than 1/3 of all the goods and services sold in the U.S. are moved through franchises.

These four successful synergisms have impacted the world in a big way, that's for sure. Certainly each of these synergisms has helped countless people create huge fortunes. But it's safe to say that only the last one on the list — franchising — is a viable means for the average person to copycat their way to wealth.

FRANCHISING: A COPYCATTERS' DREAM COME TRUE

Let's face it, very few people have the money or the brains to design and build a new computer ... or to own and operate a car dealership or a retail store selling fax machines. You can't really copycat these enterprises because they require special skills, lots of money or both.

That's the beauty of franchising. By definition, franchises are duplicatable models. If a product or service can't be duplicated, then it can't be franchised.

Franchising has been a real boon to consumers, because with a franchise, a successful product or service can be duplicated in hundreds or thousands of different locations all over the world. Again, McDonald's is a perfect example. The first restaurant was located in only one city, San Bernardino, California. Most everyone who ate there loved the McDonald brothers' low-cost hamburgers and fries. But prior to franchising, only local people could enjoy their food because there was only one location.

Through franchising, McDonald's was able to make their burgers and fries available in every city in the country. To date there are 21,000 McDonald's restaurants in 101 countries, and a new one opens somewhere in the world every two days!

If consumers are happy about the concept of franchising, just think how franchise owners and operators feel — they must be ecstatic! Obviously, for thousands of business owners, franchising is a copycatter's dream come true!

FRANCHISING: HOW IT WORKS

In effect, franchising is a proven way for people to copycat their way to wealth by duplicating a successful business. Franchising is the classic example of a successful partnership. The umbrella company — or franshisor — expands its market share by selling a proven, profitable system to an investor. The investor — or franchisee — buys a turnkey business, thereby minimizing his risk by avoiding the costly mistakes that inevitably occur with any new start-up business. It's a win/win situation.

Franchising is perhaps the greatest business success story of the 20th century. When McDonald's opened its first franchise in the mid-1950s, franchising was misunderstood and perceived by most serious investors as a scam. Today, only 50 years later, franchising is a worldwide phenomenon. Amazing!

NETWORK MARKETING: THE ULTIMATE SYNERGISM

Imagine for a moment, that you were in charge of creating the *ultimate synergism for wealth creation* — a synergism so awesome, so powerful, that it would touch every person on the planet and improve and enrich their lives in the process.

Your synergism would be so duplicatable that anyone could copycat it.

Your synergism would be so affordable that anyone could get involved.

Your synergism would grow exponentially, instead of linearly.

Your synergism would be available all over the world.

Your synergism would touch both men and women ... young and old ... rich or poor.

Your synergism would be the ultimate copycat system to create wealth.

Well, I'm delighted to report that there is such

a radical synergism! It's a match made in heaven
... the creative combination of two of the most
powerful wealth-creating vehicles in the history
of the world ... *the marriage of franchising and
exponential growth.*

The result is a concept I call the Ultimate
Synergism—Network Marketing. *What a brilliant synergistic concept — a franchise that
grows exponentially!*

Network Marketing is synergism at its best.
It's the ice cream cone ... it's the automobile ...
it's the fax machine. And mark my words, if
you thought franchising was big — *you ain't
seen nothin' yet!*

CHAPTER 7

Network Marketing:
The Ultimate Copycat System!

CHAPTER 7

Network Marketing: The Ultimate Copycat System!

I've always felt that I don't have to be an originator — just a good duplicator.

— Max Cooper, owner of 47 McDonald's franchises

So far we've agreed that duplication is the key to franchising's success, and we've agreed that exponential growth through compounding is a time-honored way to create wealth.

That's why I call Network Marketing the "ultimate synergism" — it combines the best from the *concept of franchising* ... with the best from the *concept of exponential growth*. It's a marriage made in heaven!

Let's take a few moments to review each of

these two concepts before learning how they combine to create the ultimate copycat system for wealth creation — Network Marketing!

PARABLE OF THE UNPROFITABLE SERVANT

As we pointed out earlier, exponential growth (also known as "compounding" and "the doubling concept") is a time-honored, wealth-building concept that rich people have been taking advantage of for thousands of years.

Even the Bible recognizes the importance of taking advantage of compounding, as evidenced by Jesus' parable of the "Unprofitable Servant." The parable goes like this:

The master of a large estate was preparing to leave on a long business trip. He summoned three trusted servants and gave each a sum of money for safekeeping. The first servant received five talents; the second servant, two talents; and the third servant, one talent.

The first two servants invested the money they were given, and when the master returned, they had doubled the principle and were praised by the master for their wisdom.

The third servant, however, was afraid of losing the money, so he buried it in the ground. He returned the single talent to his master, and nothing more. The master chastised the servant for not investing the money with bankers, and angrily dismissed him on the spot!

PUTTING YOUR MONEY TO WORK FOR YOU

The parable points out the importance of making wise and productive decisions, whether they be financial decisions or spiritual ones. It's not enough to be blessed with opportunity ... or money ... or talents ... or abilities ... or a soul. The real issue is what you do with those blessings — whether you bury them in the ground, so to speak, or invest them wisely so that they grow and multiply.

The power of exponential growth is obvious — you can put your money to work for you so that you double ... and re-double ... and redouble your money again and again. With compounding, your money is working for you — even while you're sleeping! Einstein knew what he was talking about when he called compounding the "8th wonder of the world!"

TIME IS AN ISSUE

There's a catch, of course. Otherwise, everybody would be copying the exponential system for wealth creation and everyone in the world would be rich, isn't that true? There are two challenges to traditional compounding —

and for most of us, they are MAJOR CHAL-
LENGES.

First, in order to invest money, we must
have extra money left over after we pay our
bills! Unfortunately, that's seldom the case.
As a comedian once put it, "Most of us have
TOO MUCH MONTH at the end of the
MONEY!" The average person is lucky to
put away $100 a month — and $1,200 a year
isn't much of a nest egg.

Second, growing your money through compounding takes time — a lot of time! It would
take more than seven years for $1,000 to double
to $2,000 if it earned 10% a year in the stock
market. The doubling concept doesn't look so
attractive when you only have a few hundred
dollars — or even a few thousand dollars — to
invest.

Frankly, most people are just too busy getting by to get rich through compounding. But
thanks to Network Marketing, *today there is a
franchise-type system that enables you to create wealth and freedom exponentially in months
and years, instead of decades!*

THE SYSTEM IS THE ANSWER

Because Network Marketing is so duplicatable, it's the ultimate copycat system for wealth

creation. It's an affordable, franchise-like concept that leaves nothing to chance. To succeed in Network Marketing, you don't have to possess "star" talent — like Tom Cruise or Whitney Houston — and you don't have to be a born genius — like Albert Einstein or Bill Gates.

Unlike the entertainment industry, Network Marketing is NOT built around a star. It's built around ordinary people getting EXTRA-ordinary results by copycatting a proven system, and then teaching others to do the same (Network Marketing has been described as "average people making above-average incomes").

But instead of spending *hundreds of thousands* of dollars to start a franchise, you only need to invest *hundreds* of dollars to start your Network Marketing "franchise"! That's why some experts are calling Network Marketing the "People's Franchise" ... and why I call it the "Alternative Franchise."™

COPYCATTING THE RIGHT PLAN

The key to building a large, profitable franchise and to building a large, profitable Network Marketing distributorship is the same — you need to take advantage of your God-given ability as a master copycatter, a talent we agree you already possess. The only difference is, with

Networking you'll copycat a franchise-type concept that creates true wealth, as opposed to copycatting the job track, which only creates temporary income.

When you invest *money* in a franchise — or when you invest *time* in a Network Marketing business — what you are really investing in is THE SYSTEM. Instead of trying to create from scratch a multi-billion dollar enterprise like McDonald's, doesn't it make more sense to follow their blueprint for success?

More than anything else, what the McDonald's Corporation offers its franchisees is a goof-proof system. People may laugh at the name of McDonald's state-of-the-art training center — it's called Hamburger University — but at McDonald's headquarters, training and education are SERIOUS business!

In order to be awarded a McDonald's franchise, you have to attend Hamburger U. and *learn to copycat their proven system* ... a system that has been working like a charm for almost 50 years! If you aren't willing to copycat the system, you don't get a franchise. It's that simple. The last thing McDonald's wants is a failed franchise!

FRANCHISING IS A WINNER

I think it's safe to say that during the 1980s

and '90s, franchising was the world's hottest business concept — and the industry is still enjoying phenomenal growth. According to *Entrepreneur* magazine, in 1996 540,000 franchises worldwide rang up sales of $758 billion. THAT'S RIGHT — $758 BILLION!

Considering that franchising was thought of as a scam only 50 years ago (and was almost banned by the U.S. Congress), it's amazing that today the industry enjoys a great reputation.

HOW NETWORK MARKETING COMPARES TO FRANCHISING

Network Marketing companies assume a role similar to successful franchises. The Networking company supports its "franchisees" (better known as distributors) by offering quality products and a turnkey system backed up by tried-and-true marketing and educational materials, such as brochures, flyers, tapes, and such.

The system is the key when it comes to both franchising and Network Marketing. Your success depends on your ability to duplicate — not innovate. The better you are at copycatting the system that already exists, the more successful you will be.

No matter when you join a Network Marketing company, you are always the head of your own company ... and each of your independent distributors is head of his or her own company. It's literally a network of CEOs.

ADVANTAGES OF NETWORKING OVER FRANCHISING

Although franchising and Networking are both copycat systems, Networking enjoys several key advantages over franchising. Take a look at this chart comparing these two proven copycat systems:

FRANCHISING	VS.	NETWORK MARKETING
Average franchise fee is $85,000	↔	Start up for $500 or less
Trade time for money (linear growth)	↔	Income grows exponentially
YOU PAY 3%-10% monthly franchising fee	↔	Company PAYS YOU 3% - 28% of your organization
Hire & fire employees	↔	No employees
Overhead grows as you grow	↔	Home-based business
Store hrs. are your hrs.	↔	Set your own hours
Restricted territory	↔	National & global territory
Building someone else's dream!	↔	Building your own dream!

As you can see, Network Marketing takes the best from franchising — the concept of a duplicatable system — and leaves the rest. As a result, Networking takes Copycat Marketing to a whole new level, which is why some experts are calling Network Marketing "the next step in the evolution of free enterprise."

FRANCHISE WITH EXPONENTIAL GROWTH

Like a franchisee, each distributor in your network owns their own business, distributing products and building a network of distributors. But unlike franchisees, as a Network Marketer you do NOT have to stay in the role of a franchisee. You can choose to *play the role of the franchisor* by sponsoring other people into your business and teaching them to copycat a proven system for wealth creation.

In other words, franchisees will always be locked into linear growth, no matter how many franchises they own. Let me explain by describing a couple of scenarios.

In the first scenario, let's assume you are the owner of six franchises. This is what the *linear growth chart* for your franchise-based business would look like:

(grows linearly)

No matter how many additional franchises you acquire, the growth will always be linear. Which means you can never earn more than the total profits of your six franchises.

In the second scenario, let's assume you're heading up a growing network of independent distributors. Over a period of time you have sponsored six key distributors and duplicated yourself by teaching them to copycat you by sponsoring six key distributors. Each one of these six key distributors copycats the system and sponsors six key distributors, and so on down the line. This is what the *exponential growth chart* for your Networking business would look like:

Network Marketer

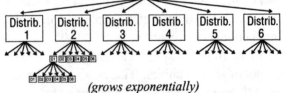

(grows exponentially)

As you can plainly see, by sponsoring six distributors and teaching your new people to copycat what you did throughout your organization, you'd be leveraging your business with hundreds of "Alternative Franchises"™ (versus only six traditional franchises).

And that's only the tip of the iceberg! When the doubling concept of exponential growth starts to kick in, the growth becomes explosive. Because of the power of exponential growth, some Network Marketers have organizations that number in the thousands — even the hundreds of thousands!

Imagine earning an override commission on the wholesale product volume generated by each of those distributors. It's little wonder that some Network Marketers live lifestyles of the rich and famous!

YOU GET PAID FOR RECOMMENDING!

We all know that the best kind of advertising is word-of-mouth advertising, isn't that true? It's something we do all the time. If we see a great movie, like *Forrest Gump*, we recommend it to our friends. But do we get paid when our friends go to see it? NO, of course not!

Same goes for recommending a great restaurant. We tell our friends and family when we eat at a terrific restaurant — but does the owner give us a commission on our friends' dinner tab? NO WAY!

In Network Marketing, you get paid a commission for recommending products and services that you use and recommend anyway. It's a win/win situation — and it's the most effective, most ethical kind of marketing in the world.

HOW NETWORK MARKETING WORKS

You know, McDonald's didn't start off with 20,000-plus restaurants all over the world. They started off with just one restaurant— and then opened another restaurant just like the first one. And that's how you can start creating exponential growth through Network Marketing — you start with just you and one other person.

Do you think it would be possible for you to find just one person each month to join you in your business? Just one partner who's interested in more freedom, recognition, happiness and security ... one partner who's interested in improving his life, and the lives of his family?

One good person a month — that's all it takes!

HOW ONE PERSON A MONTH CAN GROW TO 4,096

Once you "sponsor" that person into your Network, you become his or her coach. You don't need to concentrate all your efforts on selling your company's products. You must teach and coach your new person to effectively copycat the system.

Now, in month two, you teach your first new

person how to copycat what you did and sponsor one person, while you sponsor another new person. So, at the end of month two, you've personally sponsored two people and your first new person has sponsored one, as well. Now you have a group of four — you and three others, isn't that correct?

Then you keep copycatting your sponsor's success system and teach your new partners to copy you, too, for month three ... four ... five ... and so on. By the end of your first year, you'll have personally sponsored 12 people — one each month. And each one of them has sponsored one person each month, as well ... and so on.

Now, at the end of one year, let's look at how the tremendous power of *exponential growth* combined with a simple, duplicatable *franchise-like concept* called Network Marketing has exploded your business:

By sponsoring just one person a month — and by having each of them copycat your efforts and sponsor one person a month — by the end of 12 months, *your organization would have 4,096 independent businesses in the form of Alternative Franchises!*

Here's the really exciting part — the company pays you a percentage of your organizational sales volume. If the Network Marketing company only pays 3% to 28% in sales commissions, you would earn between $12,000 and $20,000 PER MONTH — or more!

That, my friend, is HOW TO COPYCAT YOUR WAY TO WEALTH!

The Undisputed Facts about Network Marketing

We've talked a lot about the theory behind Network Marketing. Now let's look at some of the facts about this dynamic industry. First of all, Network Marketing, like franchising, is a 50-year-old industry. It's a powerful, efficient method of distributing products and services from the manufacturer to the consumer.

Today Network Marketing is an established way of doing business in 125 countries, and worldwide approximately 20 million people are independent distributors with a Networking company.

Follow the Leader

In evaluating any industry, you need to look at the leader, because the speed of the leader equals the speed of the pack: Microsoft in computer software ... Coca-Cola in non-alcoholic beverages ... and so on. Both of these companies are leading their industries into phenomenal growth cycles.

In Network Marketing, the industry leader is far and away the Amway Corporation of Ada, Michigan. Amway has more than 2.5 million renewing distributors in over 75 countries and territories, with foreign sales accounting for two-thirds of Amway's total sales. Amway Japan is the fastest-growing foreign-owned company in Japan, second in size and profitability only to Coca-Cola. Worldwide, Amway did $5.3 billion in 1994; $6.3 billion in 1995; $6.8 billion in 1996, and is currently growing at 19% per annum — that's more than $1 billion per year!

How big is Amway? In the giant household and personal products industry, Amway ranks second behind Proctor & Gamble in annual revenues — and ahead of Fortune 500 mainstays Colgate-Palmolive and Johnson & Johnson!

It's obvious — Network Marketing is no longer a theory. It is no longer controversial. Today Network Marketing is where franchising was 20 years ago — it's a "people's franchise concept" that grows exponentially, and it's just entering its peak growing phase!

GROWING BY LEAPS AND BOUNDS

The industry has enjoyed phenomenal growth during the past few years. When I first started writing about the industry in the early 1990s,

Networking was a $20 billion dollar a year business. Since that time it has grown at a rate of 10% a year, and it reached worldwide sales of $100 billion in 1996. And the best news is the BIG GROWTH is still ahead, as illustrated by this graph:

NETWORK MARKETING GROWTH CHART

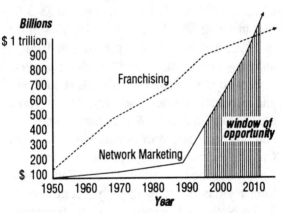

As this growth chart clearly shows, today we are just starting to enter the Golden Age of Network Marketing. Networking is today where franchising was 20 years ago — which means *the best is yet to come!* I predict that because of Network Marketing's exponential advantage, the industry is poised to surpass franchise sales sometime during the next decade.

This is more than a major trend — this is a worldwide MOVEMENT! I call it the E^2 Movement. E^2 stands for "Exponential Entrepreneur," and Network Marketing is perfectly positioned to take advantage of a tidal wave of home-based entrepreneurism that is sweeping the globe!

The question you need to ask yourself is this: *"Am I going to be one of the people who watches Network Marketing explode over the next decade? ... Or am I going to be one of the people who helps make it explode — and profits in the process?"*

Conclusion

It's Your Turn!

Conclusion

It's Your Turn!

An invasion of armies can be resisted.
But not an idea whose time has come.
— Victor Hugo

The best way to wrap up a book about copycatting is to tell you a story about one of nature's best copycatters — the Processionary Caterpillar. These fascinating little insects get their name from their curious habit of traveling in an orderly procession, one after the other.

Processionary Caterpillars are great at copycatting the behavior of their fellow caterpillars. In fact, copycatting is all they know how to do. Their "herd instinct" is so powerful they've been known to follow each other, one after the other, end-to-end, for miles at a time.

Years ago a scientist in France conducted an informal experiment to test the strength of the Processionary Caterpillar's herd instinct. He placed several caterpillars on the rim of a large flowerpot filled to the brim with the caterpillars' favorite leafy food source and an abundance of fresh water.

Sure enough, the caterpillars began following the lead caterpillar around and around the rim of the flower pot. They marched ahead without pause ... hour after hour ... day after day.

Amazingly, food and water were inches away from the caterpillars. Yet their instinct to follow was so strong, not a single one of the Processionary Caterpillars would break formation. After seven days of endless marching, all of the caterpillars died from exhaustion.

WHO ARE YOU CHOOSING TO COPYCAT?

Like the Processionary Caterpillar, we humans have a strong herd instinct, too. That's why we're such great copycatters. Fortunately for us, our herd instinct is counter-balanced by our ability to think. Because we can think and reason, we can make choices, whereas insects are totally at the mercy of their instincts.

Unlike the Processionary Caterpillar, humans can choose to break away from the herd. We can choose to stop copycatting people whose system will lead us to debt ... dependence ... doubt ... and, for all too many people, DISASTER! Or we can choose to start copycatting people whose system will lead us to prosperity and abundance.

What about you? Are you like the Processionary Caterpillar, blindly copycatting the plan of the caterpillar in front of you until you end up like 95% of the "human Processionary Caterpillars" — dead ... dead broke ... or barely getting by on a government pension?

Or are you willing to break away from the herd and become a 5%-er by copycatting a proven plan that could lead to true wealth?

WHY COPYCAT A SYSTEM FOR WEALTH CREATION?

Why should you break ranks and copycat a system that creates wealth? That question can be answered in one word — FREEDOM!

Freedom from debt, once and for all.

Freedom from a boss looking over your shoulder.

Freedom from taking part-time jobs to make ends meet.

Freedom to set your own hours — and your own vacation schedule!

Freedom to build your dream, instead of someone else's dream!

And freedom from full-time stress caused by too much work for too little money.

True wealth, you'll remember, is having enough money and enough time to do WHAT you want, WHEN you want.

True wealth puts the word FREE back into FREE ENTERPRISE. And that, my friend, more than any other single reason, is why we must copycat a system for creating true wealth.

It's Your Turn

You can do it — you have all the skills needed to succeed in Network Marketing because you were born a master copycatter! It's time to choose to break ranks with the 95%-ers and start copycatting a system that creates wealth for YOU, instead of continuing to copycat the caterpillars going around and around in an endless circle.

It's your turn to break out of the pack and begin creating true wealth and total freedom!

The simple truth is, you're not required to do anything that you're not already doing! You're already an expert at copycatting, isn't that true? So don't you think it's time to copycat a system that will help you **realize your dreams**, instead of a system that makes you **compromise your dreams**?

It's obvious!

WHAT ARE YOUR REAL FEARS ABOUT THE FUTURE?

There's nothing to fear about copycatting a system that creates true wealth. *THE REAL FEAR* is ending up like 95% of the people in this world — dead, dead-broke, or dependent on family, church or state.

The real fear is to retire in your "Golden Years" on a poverty-level pension.

The real fear is to settle for living a life of mediocrity, when you know in your heart that you are capable of so much more.

The real fear is giving up on your dreams because you've chosen to copycat a plan that can never make them come true.

My friend, you must NEVER let negative people steal your dreams! Negative people are like Processionary Caterpillars — they will insist you copycat their system, living from paycheck to paycheck, even if it leads around and around in an endless circle.

OPPORTUNITIES ARE NEVER MISSED ...

It's your turn to be free by creating true

wealth, but you have to start copycatting a different plan. Always remember, you have to seize opportunities when they are presented to you, not when you think you are ready for them.

Like I always say, *"Opportunities are never missed. Someone else just takes advantage of them first!"*

Don't let this opportunity pass you by. This is your chance to grab the brass ring. You can do it. You're already a great copycatter. Give yourself a chance to cash in on the greatest economic movement since franchising.

Networking is today where franchising was 20 years ago — it's a $100-billion-per-year business that is destined to explode to $700 billion in the next decade!

Don't wait any longer! There has never been a better time to get involved! Today you can position yourself at the beginning of a worldwide movement. It's your turn to become a 5%-er. So take advantage of this opportunity before someone else does.

You're a great copycatter.

You have the skills it takes to succeed.

The timing couldn't be better.

You deserve it.

It's your turn ... to copycat your way to wealth!